Positive Affirmations Vision Board Clip Art Book: Empower Toolkit Series

Welcome to The Empower Toolkit Series: Positive Affirmations Vision Board & Clip Art Book! This edition is packed with over 175 inspirational affirmation cards designed for both men and women.

This book is your creative playground, filled with:
- Inspiring images
- Affirmations
- Empowering quotes

Designed to help you:
- Manifest your dreams
- Embrace your fullest potential

Whether you envision financial freedom, career success, or personal growth, this book is your companion on the journey to greatness.

Dive into pages brimming with:
- Vibrant clip art
- Symbols of wealth and abundance
- Uplifting pictures, phrases, and words

Let your imagination soar as you craft a vision board that reflects your unique aspirations and celebrates your beautiful, unstoppable self.

Get ready to:
- Turn your dreams into reality
- Empower yourself
- Prosper

Your journey to empowerment and prosperity starts here!

How to Create a Vision Board: A Quick Guide

Materials Needed:

Poster board or corkboard

Magazines and printables

Scissors

Glue sticks or Mod Podge

Markers and pens

Stickers and decorative items

Personal photos

Tape or push pins (optional)

Steps to Create Your Vision Board:

Define Your Goals:

Reflect on what you want to achieve in areas like career, personal growth, health, relationships, and travel.

Gather Your Materials:

Collect all the listed materials and set up a comfortable workspace.

Find Inspiring Images and Words:

Cut out or print images and words that represent your goals.
Prepare Your Base:

Arrange your images on the board before gluing or pinning them.
Affix Items to Your Board:

Glue or pin your images and words onto the board.
Add Personal Touches:

Write specific goals, affirmations, or quotes on the board.
Display Your Vision Board:

Place it in a spot where you'll see it daily.
Review and Update:

Regularly review and update your vision board as your goals evolve.
Conclusion:
A vision board helps visualize and manifest your dreams. With creativity and the right materials, you can create a motivating tool to keep your goals in focus. Start today and see your aspirations come to life!

I am friendly

Be yourself

I am proud of who I am

I am proud of the color of my skin

I am bold and will not apologize for it.

I am capable of Patience

I will not allow negativity to affect my self-worth

I am generous

I RESPECT MYSELF

I WILL STRIVE TO BE OPEN MINDED

I INSPIRE OTHERS

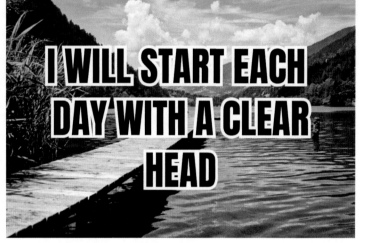

I WILL START EACH DAY WITH A CLEAR HEAD

I DEFINE MYSELF

TODAY WILL BE A GREAT DAY BECAUSE I CHOOSE TO BE POSITIVE

I WILL LOOK FOR JOY IN THE SIMPLE THINGS IN LIFE

I DESERVE TO FEEL BETTER THAN I DO TODAY.

I AM STILL LEARNING, MISTAKES ARE PART OF THE PROCESS.

STUMBLING BLOCKS BECOME STEPPING STONES.

MY DREAMS ARE MINE TO REACH.

HAPPINESS IS THE KEY TO FREEDOM

I HAVE SOMETHING TO OFFER THIS WORLD

EVERY DAY IS A NEW DAY, FILLED WITH NEW POSSIBILITIES.

GOOD THINGS ALWAYS COME IF YOU ARE PATIENT

I am not rude	I am Joyful
I am worthy of Validation	I am Powerful
I am Smart and Clever	I approve of me
I am confident	My shyness is not is not a sign of weakness

MY CHILDHOOD DOES NOT DEFINE ME.

SOMETIMES HEALING HURTS.

SOME DAYS ITS OK TO STAY IN BED.

MY THOUGHTS MATTER.

IT'S OK TO BE SAD.

MY EMOTIONS ARE JUSTIFIED.

IT'S HOW I REACT THAT MATTERS.

MY BAD DAYS WON'T LAST FOREVER.

I WILL KEEP TRYING EVEN WHEN IT LOOKS HOPELESS.

I CAN GET THROUGH THIS, I CAN GET THROUGH ANYTHING.

I WILL NOT LET MY FEAR CONTROL ME.

I DESERVE TO TAKE A BREAK WHENEVER I NEED ONE.

I WILL NOT LET MY ANXIETIES TAKE OVER.

i AM ALLOWED TO MAKE ROOM IN MY LIFE FOR GREATER THINGS.

I DESERVE TO HAVE PEACE OF MIND

I HAVE THE POWER TO CONTROL MY EMOTIONS

I WILL SET HEALTHY BOUNDARIES & HONOR THEM.

IT'S OK IF I
FEEL FEAR
SOMETIMES.

IT'S OK IF I
FEEL SAD
SOMETIMES.

IT'S OK IF I
DON'T HAVE
ALL THE
ANSWERS

I CHOOSE TO
SEE THE
BEAUTY IN
THIS WORLD.

I CHOOSE
NOT BE
JUDGEMENTAL

I CHOOSE TO
BE SMART

I AM PROUD
OF MY
HERITAGE

I AM PROUD
OF MY LINEAGE

I AM PROUD
OF WHO I AM

I AM MENTALLY STRONG.

I AM PHYSICALLY STRONG.

I AM MENTALLY CAPABLE.

I AM AN ASSET.

calm your mind

I AM A GIVING PERSON.

MY BODY IS DIVINE.

MY SOUL IS PURE.

I AM WORTHY AND VALUABLE.

I AM FABULOUS.

I RADIATE GOOD VIBES.

I RADIATE POSITIVITY.

I DESERVE FRIENDS.

I DESERVE TIME FOR MYSELF.

I DESERVE SLEEP

I DESERVE REST AND RELAXATION.

I DESERVE ALONE TIME.

I AM ONE IN EIGHT BILLION.

I WILL NOT APOLOGIZE FOR MY CONFIDENCE.

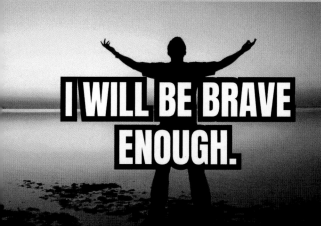

I WILL BE BRAVE ENOUGH.

I WILL NOT BE AFRAID TO ASK FOR HELP.

I WILL NOT BE AFRAID TO ASK FOR HELP.

I WILL BE CALM EVEN WHEN I AM SURROUNDED BY CHAOS

I WILL BE CALM EVEN WHEN I AM SURROUNDED BY CHAOS

I WILL LAUGH DAILY, EVEN ON DAYS FILLED WITH SADNESS.

It's OK I DON'T KNOW IT ALL, NO ONE DOES.

MY BEST IS ENOUGH.

IF MY KIDS SEE ME CRY, THAT'S OKAY.

I AM NOT MY PARENTS

I CAN CHOOSE BETWEEN RIGHT & WRONG.

I AM CAPABLE OF LOVE AND BEING LOVED.

I AM NO ONE'S PRISONER.

I HAVE THE POWER TO CONTROL MY ACTIONS

I CAN GET BACK UP EVEN WHEN I FALL.

I AM RESPECTFUL OF OTHER PEOPLE'S FEELINGS

I AM GRATEFUL. FOR MY FAMILY.

I AM GRATEFUL. FOR MY SPOUSE.

I AM GRATEFUL FOR MY STRENGTH.

I AM GRATEFUL FOR THE GIFT OF LIFE.

AM GRATEFUL FOR MY CHILDREN.

I AM GRATEFUL FOR MY FAITH.

I AM GRATEFUL FOR MY BUSINESS.

I am open to financial abundance.

I lead with integrity, vision, and compassion.

I deserve and enjoy life's luxuries.

Luxury is a natural part of my life.

I attract luxurious experiences

Prosperity & wealth are my constant companions

I am grateful for the financial abundance in my life.

I am a confident and inspiring employer

I am worthy of financial abundance & success.

I am confident in my ability to achieve my financial goals.

Money flows easily and effortlessly into my life.

Money brings freedom and opportunities.

My talents and skills create endless opportunities for success.

I save wisely, securing my future

I am open to receiving wealth in all forms

I am steadily paying off my debts, achieving financial freedom.

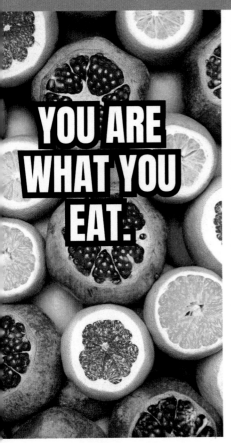

YOU ARE WHAT YOU EAT.

EAT WELL FEEL GOOD.

IT'S NEVER TOO LATE TO START.

HEALTHY LIFESTYLE

LOVE YOUR BODY

HEALTH IS WEALTH.

Stop doing what doesn't work

YOU GOT THIS!

YOU CAN DO IT!

YOU ARE UNSTOPPABLE.

I AM PROUD OF MYSELF.

F I T N E S S

W O R K O U T

FOCUS!

YOU ARE STRONG.

TAKE A BREAK!

TAKE A BREAK!

I ATTRACT OPPORTUNITIES TO TRAVEL.

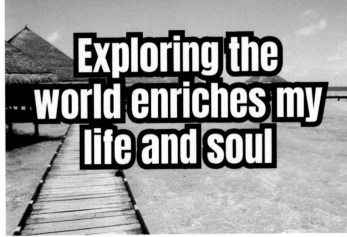
Exploring the world enriches my life and soul

I AM A WORLD TRAVERLER!

YOU DID IT!

I embrace the diversity and beauty of the world through travel.

I AM OPEN TO NEW ADVENTURES.

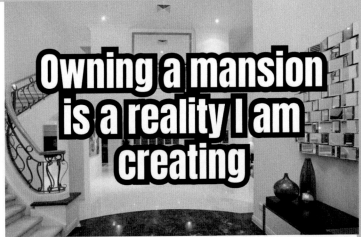

I am worthy of living in a beautiful mansion

Owning a mansion is a reality I am creating

My dream mansion provides comfort and joy.

I attract luxury and abundance .

My mansion is a reflection of my success.

I deserve an elegant mansion.

I will buy my dream home.

I am grateful for my luxurious, home.

KNOW YOUR WORTH.

PEACE OF MIND

LITTLE STEPS MATTER.

TRUST YOUR VISION.

DO YOUR THING!

RADIATE GOOD ENERGY.

STAY STRONG, AND POWER ON.

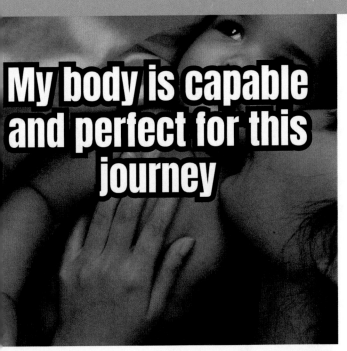

My body is capable and perfect for this journey

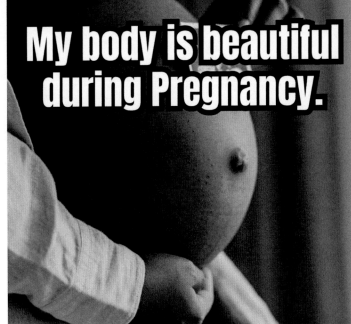

My body is beautiful during Pregnancy.

I am nurturing a healthy and strong baby.

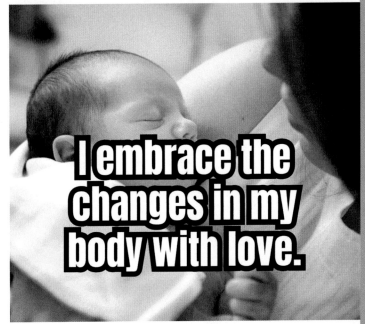

I embrace the changes in my body with love.

I AM SO GRATEFUL FOR YOU.

MY BUNDLE OF JOY!

My luxury car reflects my success.

I deserve to drive a luxurious car.

I am grateful for my luxury car.

I attract wealth for luxury vehicles.

I deserve luxurious, high-performance cars.

conclusion, the Positive Affirmations Vision Board & Clip Art Book, The Empower Toolkit Series, is powerful for manifesting your dreams. With over 175 affirmation cards and inspiring visuals, it empowers you to embrace positivity and take actionable steps toward a fulfilling and successful life.

Made in the USA
Las Vegas, NV
30 November 2024

13016660R00033

TODAY IS A NEW BEGINNING

just go

HAPPY MIND HAPPY LIFE.

UNLOCK YOUR POTENTIAL

BE YOUR OWN HERO

NEW MINDS NEW RESULT

THINK ABOUT THINGS DIFFERENTLY

$ Side Hustle

YOU BECOME WHAT YOU BELIEVE.

DECIDE
COMMIT
FOCUS
SUCCEED

DO MORE OF WHAT MAKES YOU HAPPY.

REAL LOVE NEVER FAILS

NEVER GIVE UP! GREAT THINGS TAKE TIME!

START MY OWN BUSINESS

Life Skills English

Student Workbook